Helping Kids Manage Grief, Fear and Anger

Terri Akin
David Cowan
Susanna Palomares
Dianne Schilling

Write to: Innerchoice Publishing
P.O. Box 1185
Torrance, CA 90505
Email: jalmarpress@att.net
Telephone: (310) 816-3085 Fax: (310) 816-3092

ISBN 1-56499-040-0

Printed in the United States of America.
Printing #: 10 9 8 7 6 5 4 3 2 1

Contents

GRIEF ACTIVITIES

FEAR ACTIVITIES

ANGER ACTIVITIES

Introduction

This book is about three formidable feelings grief, fear and anger. Children cannot be protected from them and they can t be immunized against them. At various points in their young lives, they will suffer the loss of goals, hopes, dreams, friendships, pets and people. They will fear failure, abandonment, punishment, rejection and countless real and imaginary threats to their safety and security. And there will be no ducking their wrath. They will spend countless hours reacting in anger to siblings, peers, authority figures and themselves.

Grief, fear and anger are significant emotions so weighty in fact that they often drive children to think irrational thoughts and engage in unreasonable behaviors. Such responses left unchecked can easily spiral into destructive actions.

If we want children to succeed in life, we must equip them with the tools to manage these intense feelings. Grief, fear and anger are annoyingly persistent companions, popping up regularly throughout life.

While grief, fear and anger are perhaps the most difficult emotions to manage, children experience many others as well. They feel happy, joyous, jealous, puzzled, frustrated, anxious, bored, curious, confident, excited, eager, and just plain good or bad. Feelings are the door to experience. If a child goes through the door a thousand times a day, he or she is stamped a thousand times by feelings.

Feelings link children to their environment, their bodies, their thoughts, and their memories. Feelings tell children about conditions around them and the state of their physical and mental well-being. Feelings also shape the way children behave. This link between feelings and behavior is one of the main reasons *Helping Kids Manage Grief, Fear and Anger* was written.

Because feelings play such an important role in shaping behavior, in order to manage and change behavior children must first learn to manage feelings. And before they can manage feelings, they must understand them. *Helping Kids Manage Grief, Fear and Anger* is about understanding, managing, and learning from feelings. It is a collection of activities designed to help children explore, understand and express their feelings in safe and acceptable ways.

More than anything else, this book is a resource for teachers and counselors who want to help children develop sound self-management skills, including the ability to take charge of difficult feelings and the behaviors they produce. The book s sequential activities provide the foundational information and skill practice that children need to develop healthy responses to intense and sometimes overwhelming feelings.

Important concepts pertaining to feelings

Feelings are powerful motivators, propelling individuals to perform thousands of actions in hundreds of different ways as they respond to themselves, others and daily events. Whether good or bad, actions are always driven by feelings.

Humanity in general has shown itself rather ignorant of the meaning, control, and effective utilization of emotional experience. This lack of understanding has resulted in unnecessary widespread human misery. Individually, we tend to fare a bit better. Teachers and counselors, for example, know that a child s inability to control and manage feelings in the classroom can have destructive effects, and routinely take steps to prevent emotional outbursts from damaging relationships, property, and the climate of learning.

Whether feelings are pleasant and positive or unpleasant and negative, they are inherently *morally neutral* and, as such, cannot be labeled good or bad, right or wrong, in an ethical sense. Feelings are the natural way we all have of obtaining vital information about whatever conditions we are in. Feelings just *are!* Children need to learn that they are not good people when they experience positive feelings, such as joy and satisfaction. At the same time, they are not bad people when they experience negative emotions, such as fear and anger. It is natural and normal to experience both positive and negative feelings.

Children do, however, need an awareness of their feelings in order to develop the skills necessary to effectively manage their behavior. When children are self-observant and acknowledge the reality of their feelings, reason can be effectively applied to a situation and appropriate actions chosen. As they learn to understand and manage the feelings that produce behavior, children begin to realize that they choose, and are responsible for, their behavior. While the emotions and feelings that drive behavior are neither good nor bad, right nor wrong, the resulting behavior whether constructive or destructive is judged for its effects or moral consequences. Everyone, including all but the youngest child, is accountable for his or her actions.

The Importance of sharing and discussion

The classroom is an excellent place for children to safely explore and get to know their emotions. When they truly understand the value of feelings, children are able to function more effectively in every aspect of school and personal life. *Helping Kids Manage Grief, Fear and Anger* provides activities designed to produce these results.

The first step in learning about feelings is developing the ability to articulate them. One of this book s primary areas of focus is communication. In order for students to develop into healthy self-confident adults, they need plenty of opportunities to talk about their feelings in a safe, accepting environment.

Discussion of negative feelings is as important as talking about positive feelings. If students think their feelings of anger, hate, aggression, or hostility are unnatural or bad, they may reach the conclusion that *they* are unnatural or bad. Sharing helps children recognize that they are not the only ones with negative feelings. At one time or another we all feel angry, hurt, sad, embarrassed, jealous and frightened. These are natural, common responses. Our feelings make us human and *all* feelings are okay. The process of exploring and expressing feelings helps students learn to cope. Sometimes expression alone can defuse much of the tension produced by strong negative feelings.

Students derive many additional benefits from talking about their feelings as well as from listening when others discuss feelings. For example, through sharing and discussion, negative emotions can be defused before they are acted out in potentially destructive ways.

Finally, children learn to recognize and distinguish between various kinds of feelings, and to use their feelings to improve the richness and quality of their lives.

Remember that feelings are the lenses through which children view and interpret reality. They can become powerful tools for developing self-control and personal mastery. Through acceptance and understanding of feelings, *Helping Kids Manage Grief, Fear and Anger* teaches children to

3

take charge of situations that would normally take charge of them. This is the essence of self-management. How we support the emotional development and self-management of our students will significantly impact their social, emotional, and academic potential now and well into their adult years.

Feelings and stress

Feelings alert children to stressful events and conditions in their lives. To some degree, anything that is perceived as having emotional content related to fear, anger or sadness produces stress. Stress is generated by the same mechanisms that produce feelings, and uncomfortable feelings are the means by which children are able to identify stress. If children develop the habit of repressing uncomfortable feelings, they inhibit awareness of stress in their lives.

Feelings associated with stress exist to warn children that something in their life needs attention. If they deny or repress these feelings, that warning goes unheeded. And failing to heed stress warnings affects not only their health, but their performance. Unattended stress shuts down major components of cognitive functioning, hampering thinking and curtailing learning. Children who are chronically stressed but have little understanding of how to manage associated feelings are at serious risk. Their lives may be completely out of control. Everything suffers academics, relationships, health and quality of life.

Considerable research has demonstrated a strong relationship between the emotional development and the educational performance of children. Studies suggest that academic achievement is significantly influenced by emotions. It stands to reason that students who are preoccupied with extreme negative feelings, and the stress and tension that accompany them, are not fully engaged in learning. One role of teachers and counselors is to help children learn about, express, and manage these distressing feelings.

The ability to understand and manage feelings is fundamental to managing stress. The inability to understand and manage feelings inhibits learning. And if the detrimental effects on health and learning aren t enough, unmanaged stress also shuts down the ability to think through appropriate behavioral responses in social situations and can lead to conflict in the classroom and on the playground.

4

Repressing feelings

Societies have always been organized in part to restrict the free expression of human impulses and drives. Restrictions have traditionally been placed on individuals by those in authority to keep behavior within acceptable bounds. If schools and classrooms are to run smoothly, children must learn appropriate ways to express the feelings these impulses and drives produce.

When a child s impulses conflict with the rules and restrictions of society, the child anticipates possible danger and experiences feelings of anxiety. Since anxiety is an extremely disagreeable feeling, the child, having only a fuzzy, budding comprehension of what is happening, automatically inhibits the natural impulses and drives that produced the anxiety. This unconscious suppression of an impulse or behavior, and the feelings and thoughts that go with it, is called *repression*.

Repression of behaviors that are contrary to social norms is important to the maintenance of the broad social structure, but too often children learn to needlessly repress much of their life experience. They choose the course of routine repression in order to maintain their own social structure and to be seen as acceptable by others, particularly those in authority like parents and teachers. If children perceive that their behavior is unacceptable, they begin to see *themselves* as unacceptable. To avoid this, they become skilled at repressing unacceptable behavior and all the thoughts and feelings that go with it. Developing this habit of repression operates to their detriment from the day it begins. It takes away a vital means by which children explore and define much of what life offers them. More importantly, children can learn to repress not only the things they perceive to be unacceptable, but things that are unpleasant or uncomfortable as well. With this in mind, it is important to recognize that when children are acting out of control, they may well be struggling with irrational or automatic responses to feelings. As a teacher or counselor, you have an opportunity to help children think through both the feelings and the behavior to facilitate growth and develop control. Attacking either the behavior or the child can only promote repression and spawn new and perhaps even more detrimental behaviors.

Responding to crisis situations

Although the majority of activities in this book are intended to serve as preventive tools, you will undoubtedly face an occasional crisis or emotional overreaction and need to make a direct intervention. Most of the activities can be used in crisis situations to help kids become centered and better focused, opening avenues to discussion, communication and understanding.

What to do in a crisis:

1. Listen.

Listening may prove the most valuable helping behavior of all in crisis situations. Encouraging students to release their feelings and articulate their fear, anger and sadness will help them begin to manage whatever situation they face.

2. Validate feelings and the reality of the child s experience.

Listen *actively*, responding with statements that clearly demonstrate your understanding and acceptance of the child s feelings. This is very difficult for you. I can see how upset you are. You re very angry about what happened. I imagine that you miss your father very much. It s normal to be frightened in a situation like this.

3. Encourage expression of both thoughts and feelings.

Help the child make a distinction between thoughts, feelings and behaviors. For example, say: I understand that you *feel* very angry why do you *think* this is happening? or You are afraid that something terrible is going to happen. What does that make you want to *do*?

4. Encourage journaling.

Children who can write should be encouraged to express their feelings in a journal, diary or some other private place. Writing about difficult experiences (and the feelings generated by them) brings clarity, objectivity and a sense of relief. When children put their thoughts on paper, they do not have to keep mulling them over. Having a quiet mind reduces stress and allows children to better manage the crisis situation.

5. Activate a supportive, structured social network.

Help create a caring, supportive environment by encouraging interaction between the child and his/her peers. If the crisis is shared by several students (*e.g.*, death of a classmate) this can be accomplished through any number of group activities (discussion, writing, art, etc.). If only one child is in crisis (*e.g.*, death of a parent), one of the most effective ways is to lead a series of *Sharing Circles* using relevant topics. The Sharing Circle is an exceptionally effective teacher/counselor-led small group discussion in which children respond to a preset topic. (See *The Sharing Circle Handbook*, Innerchoice Publishing, 1992.)

6. Observe and honor appropriate rituals.

Rituals help bring closure to difficult situations. Encourage children to participate in memorial services and other formal observances. Respect individual customs relating to dress and conduct. Make sure that the child s peers understand and respect them, too.

Caution: Exercise restraint when validating and encouraging the expression of anger and fear (items 2 and 3, above). Repeated overly empathic responses can unintentionally reinforce and intensify a child s angry or fearful feelings, rather than relieve and resolve them.

Facilitate the stages of grieving

Children, like adults, must go through a fairly predictable grieving process, experiencing the stages of loss identified by Elisabeth Kubler-Ross in her groundbreaking book *On Death and Dying*.

At first, grieving children will be in a state of shock, unable to believe what is happening. They may say things like, Why me? and This can t be true, while denying the reality of the situation. In most cases, shock and disbelief soon change to anger. Children may want to blame someone or strike out in some way. Next they may experience glimmers of hope and try to bargain with parents, peers, themselves or God by promising to do things differently in exchange for the return of whatever or whomever they lost. When they realize that the situation can t be controlled, they will probably feel frustrated, which may lead to a desire to isolate themselves. Depression usually follows and is a normal reaction. Eventually children will come to terms with the reality of the situation and accept the loss. Most people, children included, cycle through these stages over and over, experiencing a tumult of emotions for quite some time long after they ve understood and accepted the situation. Birthdays and holidays are especially apt to generate renewed grieving.

To facilitate a child s grieving progress, encourage the expression of feelings. Allow time for healing, and be available and supportive during transitions from one stage to another. Social recognition and support are primary keys to healthy recovery. Again, the Sharing Circle is exceptionally well suited to this process.

How to use the activities

Ideally, *Helping Kids Manage Grief, Fear and Anger* should be implemented as a sequential program of study. For this reason, activities are arranged in a recommended order of use. However, the book may also be regarded as a general resource of ideas and activities to help students understand and manage the range of feelings they experience on a day-to-day basis.

The first section of the book consists of preliminary activities that deal with feelings in general. Use them as mental and emotional warm-up activities, much as you use limbering-up exercises to prepare the body for a rigorous workout. These easy, gentle experiences prepare students by helping them acknowledge and examine a wide spectrum of feelings. Upon this foundation, gradually introduce children to activities dealing specifically with grief, fear and anger.

All of the activities in the book are designed for use with students in grades 3 through 8, in counseling, classroom, or other group situations. Since the authors are committed to individualized instruction, no grade-level designations are provided. Please select and/or adapt activities in accordance with the abilities, interests, and needs of your students.

As students complete the activities, they will enjoy repeated opportunities to explore and talk about their own feelings and behaviors, and to discuss and respond to the feelings and behaviors of others. While the experiences themselves are important, the spirit in which the activities are presented is equally important. By creating a warm, inclusive environment where feelings are accepted without judgement and where self-expression is encouraged, you will enable your students to develop not only the skills of self-management, but expanded awareness coupled with esteem and respect for themselves and others.

Preliminary Activities

9

The Write Stuff
A Vocabulary of Feelings

Objectives:

The students will:

acquaint themselves with a variety of feeling words and their meanings through discussion.

demonstrate an understanding of new feeling words through writing.

Materials:

chalkboard and chalk; a copy of the experience sheet, A Vocabulary of Feelings for each student; writing paper and pencils

Procedure:

Begin by asking the students to brainstorm all the words they can think of to describe feelings. Cover the board with these words. Ask volunteers to choose words from the list, and describe real or hypothetical situations which might cause them to feel that way. For example, a student who chooses the word *exasperated,* might say that constantly having to pick up a younger sister s dirty clothes makes her feel exasperated.

After many students have shared their situations using the words on the board, distribute the sheet, **A Vocabulary of Feelings.** Give the students several minutes to look over the words and notice any that are unfamiliar. Then ask volunteers to name unfamiliar words and discuss their meaning with the whole group.

Explain to the students that they are going to have an opportunity to practice unfamiliar words from the list. Ask them to choose five or more words which they would like to practice using and write a sentence using each in an appropriate context. Tell the students that they may use any of the following suggestions in creating their sentences:

10

1. **Use a sentence pattern:** I feel/felt (new feeling word) when (something happens/happened).

2. **If possible, change a word to an adverb by adding *ly* and use it to describe an action:** I jealously watched as my opponent received the gold medal in the 100-yard dash.

3. **Use the word in a sentence that tells why someone feels/felt that way:** The miserable woman trudged another five miles through the snow looking for a service station at which to buy gas for her stalled car.

4. **Older students may try to change a feeling word to a noun and use that word in a sentence:** deceitful-deceit, comfortable-comfort, joyous-joy, ambivalent-ambivalence, ecstatic-ecstasy.

Remind students to make sure that their feeling words fit the situations they describe in their sentences. Encourage creativity, humor, and correct usage.

When the students have completed their sentences, ask them to form pairs and to read their sentences to their partners. Invite the partners to give each other feedback. For example, have them tell which is their favorite sentence and why. Then gather the group together and invite each person to share a sentence.

Summarize the activity by asking the students to think about all the words that can be used to describe a feeling and how the meaning varies only slightly from word to word. Ask the students why they think it could be beneficial to know many different feeling words.

A Vocabulary of Feelings

abandoned
accepted
adamant
adequate
affectionate
afraid
agony
alarmed
alienated from
   others
ambivalent
annoyed
anxious
apathetic
appreciated
astounded
attractive
awed
awkward

bad
beaten
beautiful
betrayed
bewildered
bitter
blissful
bold
bored
brave
burdened

comfortable
concerned
confident
connected
cop-out, like a
cowardly
creative
curious
cut off from others

deceitful
defeated
dejected
delighted
dependent
depressed
deprived
desperate
destructive
determined
different
diffident
diminished
disappointed in
   myself
discontented
distracted
distraught
disturbed
divided
dominated
dubious

eager
ecstatic
elated
electrified
embarrassed
empty
enchanted
energetic
enjoyment
envious
evasive
evil
exasperated
excited
exhausted
exhilarated

fawning
fearful
flustered
foolish
frantic
free
friendless
frightened
frustrated
full

glad
good
grateful
gratified
greedy
grief
groovy
guilty
gullible
gutless

happy
hateful
helpful
helpless
high
homesick
honored
hopeful
hopeless
horrible
hostile
hurt
hysterical

ignored
immortal
immobilized
impatient
Imposed upon
impressed

inadequate
incompetent
inconsistent
in control
indecisive
independent
infatuated
inferior
infuriated
inhibited
insecure
insincere
inspired
intimidated
involved
isolated

jealous
joyous
judgmental
jumpy

lazy
left out
lonely
loser, like a
lovable
loving
low
loyal

manipulated
miserable
misunderstood

needy
nervous

odd
opposed
optimistic
outraged
overlooked
overwhelmed

panicked
paranoid
peaceful
persecuted
petrified
pleasant
pleased
possessive
preoccupied
pressured

quarrelsome
quiet

refreshed
rejected
relaxed
relieved
religious
remorseful
repulsive
restless
restrained
sad
satisfied
scared
screwed up
settled
sexy
shallow
shocked
shy
silly
sluggish
sorry for self
strained
stunned
stupid
sure

tempted
tense
threatened
thwarted
tired
torn
touchy
trapped
troubled

unappreciated
uncertain
uneasy
unsettled
up-tight
used

violent
vivacious
vulnerable

wishy-washy
wonderful
worried

13

A Time I Remember Feeling...
Dyad Sequence and Discussion

Objectives:

The students will:

discuss their feelings as they relate to specific topics.

begin to understand that all people experience the same feelings, but in different ways.

Materials:

chalkboard and chalk or chart paper and magic marker

Procedure:

Select 10 to 12 feeling words from the following list and write them on the chalkboard or chart paper. Choose words that are appropriate for the age and maturity of your students.

A Time I Remember Feeling...

...Mad	...Left Out	...Lonely	...Bored
...Free	...Self-conscious	...Annoyed	...Helpless
...Suspicious	...Confident	...Relieved	...Delighted
...Curious	...Overwhelmed	...Homesick	...Depressed
...Amused	...Guilty	...Loved	...Powerful
...Jealous	...Surprised	...Disgusted	..Peaceful
...Shocked	...Worthless	...Shy	...Inspired
...Appreciated	...Optimistic	...Embarrassed	...Pessimistic
...Uneasy	...Confused	...Related	...Happy
...Scared	...Unfairly Treated		

Introduce the activity by telling the students that they are going to have an opportunity to discuss a number of feelings that they experience. Have the students form groups of four and, taking their chairs with them, spread out to various areas of the room. If necessary, join a group yourself or have one group of six; however, make sure all groups contain an even number of students.

Explain to the students that they will be involved in a dyad sequence in which they talk about feelings one-to-one with each member of their group for about 4 minutes.

Ask the students to pair up with one member of their group. When the dyads are formed, ask the students to decide who will speak first and who will speak second, and to choose a topic from the list on the board. Tell the students that they will each have 1 1/2 minutes to speak to that topic. Ask the first speakers to begin. At the end of 1 1/2 minutes, signal the students to switch roles so that the second speaker can address the same topic for another 1 1/2 minutes.

At the end of the first round, have the students change partners. This is easily accomplished by asking the students who spoke first to remain seated while the students who listened first move to a new partner within their group.

Repeat the process for each subsequent round, instructing the students to choose a new topic from the list each time. Continue until each student has had a dyad discussion with every other person in his/her group. Ask the students to return to their regular seating, and encourage everyone to participate in a culminating discussion.

Discussion Questions:

1. What did you notice or learn as you talked about these feelings with your partners?
2. How did you feel during the activity?
3. What other feelings would you like to talk about?
4. What did you learn about yourself during this activity that you would feel okay sharing with us?
5. When it comes to feelings, in what ways are you like one or more of your partners? In what ways are your feelings different?

Note: A good follow-up to this activity is the experience sheet Feel Your Feelings.

Feel Your Feelings
Experience Sheet

Life includes lots of feelings. We *all* feel them. In that way, everyone is the same. But everyone is different, too. Have you ever observed several people reacting differently to the same thing? As you read the following story, notice that all of the characters have a different feeling about the same event.

The Broken Window

All the kids in the neighborhood were having a great time playing touch football out in the street until the football went sailing through Mr. and Mrs. Henry s window. After the crash, some of the kids got scared and ran away. Margie kicked the ball, so she felt responsible. She wasn t scared, just unhappy. Margie knew that she d have to be the one to apologize and offer to pay for a new window. Margie s brother, Carl, was embarrassed. He started yelling at Margie. Carl s friend, Juan, just laughed. He was relieved. I sure am glad I m not the one who kicked that ball, he said.

Just then Mr. Henry came outside. He was carrying the football. He was very angry at first. But as soon as Margie apologized, he appeared to calm down. When Margie said she would pay for the broken window, he seemed to feel even better.

Then Mrs. Henry came out of the house. She was furious. Mr. Henry told her that everything was taken care of, but she didn t seem at all relieved. I m the one who s going to have to hire a worker to fix the window, she shouted.

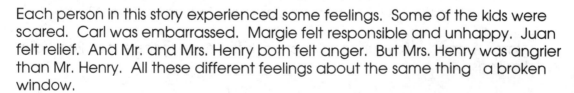

Each person in this story experienced some feelings. Some of the kids were scared. Carl was embarrassed. Margie felt responsible and unhappy. Juan felt relief. And Mr. and Mrs. Henry both felt anger. But Mrs. Henry was angrier than Mr. Henry. All these different feelings about the same thing a broken window.

How would you have felt if you had been each one of these people?

Your feelings are similar to the feelings of other people. Yet you are a one-of-a-kind person. Things that cause you to feel a certain way may cause an entirely different reaction in others. You are not exactly like everyone else.

The following exercise will help you get in touch with some of your feelings. As you write, keep in mind that *everyone* has these feelings. Feelings can be pleasant and unpleasant. But they are not good or bad. They are not right or wrong. Feelings just are!

I am happy when... _____

_____

I become angry when... _____

_____

I am sad when... _____

_____

I get scared when... _____

_____

I feel lonely when... _____

_____

I feel peaceful when... _____

_____

I become frustrated when... _____

_____

I hate it when... _____

_____

I love it when... _____

_____

17

Pantomime a Feeling
A Mime Game and Discussion

Objective:

The students will explore the roles of body language and facial expression in the communication of feelings.

Materials:

Many feeling words (such as those listed below) written separately on small sheets of paper, folded, and placed in a container. **Note:** Choose words that are appropriate for the age/maturity of your students.

relieved	rejected	satisfied	scared	embarrassed
awkward	angry	agonized	delighted	bored
indecisive	bewildered	eager	grief-stricken	tense
impatient	wishy-washy	shy	worried	insecure
mad	sorry for self	disgusted	loveable	powerful
lonely	free	confident	peaceful	silly
cowardly	surprised	hateful	tired	loving
happy	disappointed			

Procedure:

Ask the students to pair up. Have each pair draw one sheet of paper with a feeling word written on it. Direct each pair to take 5 minutes to plan a short pantomime demonstrating their feeling word. Explain that the students are to act only with their faces and bodies. They may not say words or make noises. The object is to do such a good job of pantomime that the class will be able to identify the feeling.

When the students have finished planning, have one pair at a time enact their pantomime. Enjoy, and clap after each pantomime. Then ask the group to name the feelings that the actors appeared to be demonstrating. Finally, have the actors describe to the group the situation they were acting out.

18

Discussion Questions:

After all the students have finished their pantomimes, lead a discussion by asking these and other questions:

1. Did you notice any similarities in the ways certain feelings were expressed?

2. Which feelings seem to be the easiest to read through body language and facial expression?

3. Why do our bodies and faces seem to have a language of their own?

4. What did you learn about body language by doing this activity?

Note: A good follow-up to this activity is the experience sheet Feelings and Your Body.

Feelings and Your Body
Experience Sheet

Sometimes you can figure out how other people are feeling, even if they don t tell you, right? That s because you speak the same body language as other people. If someone is shaking and sweating, with eyes wide and voice cracking, you probably conclude that the person is afraid. We can often tell what other people are feeling, even at a distance by the way they move and walk, and by the looks on their faces. And if we hear them talk, their voices give us clues, too.

Try to match the feelings and body reactions listed below. Draw a line from each feeling word to the most likely body reaction. You may decide that some feelings go with several body reactions, or vice versa. At the bottom of the page, list other feelings and body reactions you think of.

Feelings	Body Reactions
anger	tight stomach
joy	trembling jaw
excitement	slouched posture
hurt feelings	bouncy walk
confidence	pounding heart
hate	lump in throat
pride	tight jaw
nervousness	shaky arms and legs
embarrassment	frown
contentment	squeaky voice
fear	tears
grief	jittery feet
happiness	smile
love	sweaty palms
sadness	red face

_____   _____
_____   _____
_____   _____

20

The Feeling of Poetry
Creative Writing

Objectives:

The students will:

> experience the manner in which feelings spark creative endeavors.

> explore their feelings as they relate to specific sensations.

Materials:

writing materials for each student; chalk and chalkboard; stop watch or clock/watch with second hand

Procedure:

Begin by preparing a chart with five columns on the chalkboard. At the top of each column put one of these headings: **Hearing; Sight; Taste; Smell;** and **Touch**

Ask the students to pay careful attention as you read the following poems aloud. As they listen, invite the students to tune into themselves and become aware of the impressions they get   the *pictures* that come into their minds and the *feelings* they experience. Explain that one of the most important ways people use their feelings is to create things. The poems the students are about to hear evoke the sensations of rain. They are examples of written creations that were sparked by feelings.

Raindrops
Softly the rain goes pitter-patter;
Softly the rain comes falling down,
Hark to the people who hurry by,
Raindrops are footsteps from out the sky!
Softly the rain goes pitter-patter;
Softly the rain comes falling down.
> *Author unknown*

Rain
The rain is raining all around;
It falls on field and tree;
It rains on the umbrellas here
And the ships at sea.
> *Robert Louis Stevenson*

(Continued) 21

Rain in Summer

How beautiful is the rain!
After the dust and heat,
In the broad and fiery street,
In the narrow lane,
How beautiful is the rain!
How it clatters along the roofs,
Like the tramp of hoofs.

How it gushes and struggles out
From the throat of the overflowing
spout!
It pours and pours
And swift and wide,
With a muddy tide,
Like a river down the gutter roars
The rain, the welcome rain.
Henry Wadsworth Longfellow

Rain

It s raining, raining all around,
Especially in London town.
Splish, splash! of children s feet,
Running down London street.

Splash! on the window pane.
The old man gazes at the rain;
He sighs and turns away his head
And wishes he was young instead.
Pat Williams, age 13

Discussion Questions:

After you have read *each* poem, ask the students:
1. What did you hear in this poem?
2. What pictures did you see in your mind?
3. What feelings did you experience?
4. What smells did you imagine?
5. What tactile (touch) sensations did you imagine?

As the students call out responses, write their statements in the appropriate column on the chart. From time to time, reread a line or two from a poem to evoke more responses.

Finally, ask the students to write their own poems about rain (or another subject they choose). Suggest that the students borrow words and phrases from the chart as they see fit.

Conclusion:

Ask volunteers to read their poems to the class. After each poem is read, ask the class to name any feelings, sensations, and images they experienced as they listened.

Note: This is an excellent activity to do on a rainy day. If possible, open the windows and turn off the light as you read the poems and as the students write their own poems.

Tune In to Your Feelings
Experience Sheet

When you tune in to your feelings, it s the same thing as tuning into yourself. You get to know yourself better.

Have you ever gotten so wrapped up in your thoughts and the things going on around you that you forgot to tune in to your feelings? Think about a time when you said to yourself, Why did I say that? or Why did I do that? It was probably a time when you were unaware of your feelings. Usually when you know what you are feeling, you are in charge of your words and actions, too.

Think about feelings you ve experienced.
Below is a chart that lists five feelings. Read through the list and ask yourself if you have had any of these feelings lately. Put a ✔in the column that shows how often you ve had the feeling <u>during the past week</u>.

	Almost All the Time	Often	A Few Times	Hardly at All	Not at All
Pleasure					
Fear					
Amusement					
Anger					
Love					

(Continued)

23

Now write two or more sentences about each feeling. When during the past week did you feel it? What was happening? What thoughts were you having? If you checked the not at all column for a feeling, explain what you think kept you from having that feeling.

Pleasure: _____
_____
_____

Fear: _____
_____
_____

Amusement: _____
_____
_____

Anger: _____
_____
_____

Love: _____
_____
_____

TRY THIS

Keep a feelings diary. For one or two days, write down all the feelings you experience. Include as many as you can. Write where you were and what happened to bring about each feeling.

See if you can figure out whether or not you experience a lot of feelings in certain situations and very few in other situations. You may discover some interesting patterns that will help you get to know yourself better.

24

Painting Our Feelings
Art and Music Activity

Objectives:

The students will:

> express feelings through the medium of art.

> explain that they have feeling responses to external events.

Materials:

several pieces of art paper and drawing tools, with a wide selection of colors for each student; a tape player and a selection of music depicting a wide range of emotions, such as:

Sadness:

> Symphony No. 5 in E Minor,   Anton Dvorak
> Symphony No. 6 in B Minor,   Tchaikovsky

Anger:

> Night on Bare Mountain, Modest Mossorgsky
> The Sorcerer s Apprentice,   Paul A. Dukas
> The Sea (La Mer), Claude Debussy

Happiness:

> Bolero,   Maurice Ravel
> Carnival Overture,   Anton Dvorak
> Nutcracker Suite,   Tchaikovsky

Fear:

> Mercury from The Planets,   Gustav Holst
> Peer Gynt,   Edvard Grieg

Playful:

> Carnival of the Animals,   Camille Saint-Saens

Procedure:

Announce to the students that you are going to play several different musical selections. Explain that each piece has a very different feel to it and that, as you play a selection, you want the students to choose colors

(Continued)

they associate with the music and express their feelings by moving the crayons (or whatever medium is being used) across the paper. Play each selection long enough for the students to respond. Have them use a new paper for each musical selection. At the conclusion of the activity, have the students write their reactions to each musical piece on the back of the corresponding drawing.

Discussion Questions:

1. What was it like to paint your feelings? Was it easy or difficult?
2. What are some of the feelings you experienced?
3. Did the music affect how you were feeling?
4. Can you think of other external events that affect your feelings?
5. What are some events that can make you feel happy? ...sad? ...angry?

Magic Glasses
Group Experience and Discussion

Objectives:

The students will:

> describe their perceptions when observing their environment through the filter of different feelings.

> describe how negative and/or positive feelings affect their experiences.

Materials:

dime-store eye glass frames for each student (optional)

Procedure:

Have the students break into groups of four to six. Explain that you have some magic glasses that you would like the students to try on. If you are using eye glass frames, pass them out. If not, ask the students to pretend to take a pair of glasses from you and put them on. Tell the students that these are happy glasses. Now everything the students see is wonderful and joyous the whole world is a happy place. Allow about 3 minutes for the students to interact in their groups. Then, tell the students to switch to angry glasses. Again, allow about 3 minutes for interaction. Continue this process at 3-minute intervals, choosing additional feelings from the following list. End the exercise with a positive feeling.

scared	impressed	show-off	good
beautiful	shy	elated	excited
curious	confident	gloomy	brave

Discussion Questions:

1. How did things appear to you when you were wearing happy glasses? ...angry glasses? ...(other feeling) glasses?

2. Do you have days when it seems like you *really are* wearing a particular pair of feeling glasses? What happens?

3. What connection is there between how you view the world and the kinds of experiences you have?

4. What have you learned from this exercise?

27

Be Happy!
Class Discussion and Experience Sheet

Objectives:

The students will:

        interview classmates concerning what makes them happy.

        identify areas of happiness in their own lives.

Materials:

chalkboard and chalk; one copy of the experience sheet, The Keys to Happiness, for each student

Procedure:

Write the following quotation on the chalkboard. Ask a student to read it aloud.

Most people are just about as happy as they make up their minds to be.
Mark Twain

Facilitate discussion on the subject of happiness by asking these and other questions:

1. What do you think Mark Twain means when he says most people are as happy as they decide to be?
2. Do you agree with that thought? Why or why not?
3. What does happiness feel like inside?
4. What does happiness look like on the outside?
5. Do you think people have control over their feelings? Explain.

At the conclusion of the discussion, have the class divide into groups of four. Pass out the experience sheet, The Keys to Happiness, and have the students each interview two other members of their group, using the experience sheet to record responses. After giving the students time to complete the last item on the experience sheet, ask volunteers to share some of their keys to happiness with the class.

28

The Keys to Happiness
Experience Sheet

Interview two people. Discover 3 important things that bring happiness to each of them.

Name: _____

1. _____

2. _____

3. _____

Name: _____

1. _____

2. _____

3. _____

Now take some time to think about what makes *you* happy. What are the keys to your happiness? Write what they are on the keys.

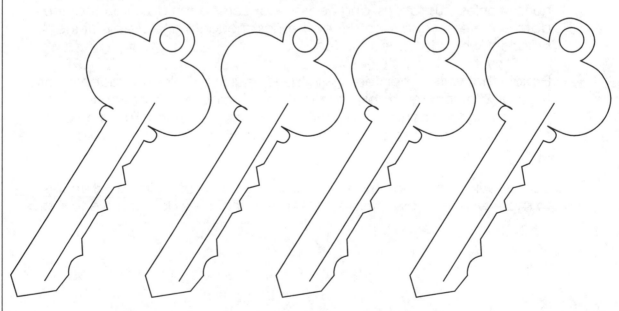

29

What s on My Mind
A Journal of Concerns

Objectives:

The students will:

write in a daily journal about their angers, frustrations, worries, annoyances, and general concerns.

share selected concerns with a group and others with the teacher or counselor.

Materials:

composition books or writing paper stapled to form a journal; pencils or pens

Procedure:

Distribute composition books or hand-made journals. Tell the students to write on the front cover, **Journal of Concerns,** plus their names. Explain to them that a journal is a good place to express and clarify feelings, especially when those feelings and concerns relate to problems. In this journal, they will have a chance to write down their gripes, annoyances, hurts, worries, frustrations, and general concerns each day. Ask that they date each entry and record their feelings, thoughts, and details of the situations which triggered the feelings.

Explain that writing their feelings in the journal may help the students learn to deal with uncomfortable situations until a solution can be found. Channeling their concerns into writing can also help them focus on a feeling without acting out or losing their temper, and can have a calming effect.

Each week, encourage the students to select one of their journal entries to share with the class. Assure the students that they do not have to share something that they would rather keep private, but explain that sharing with others may give them insights into their feelings, thoughts, and behaviors.

Invite the students to sign up for an appointment with you to share one or more concerns from their journal in private. Use active listening techniques such as paraphrasing, nodding, asking questions for clarification, and maintaining eye contact. Listening alone will help you communicate acceptance and understanding of what is important to the child. Listening will also focus the attention of students on their own needs and will help them develop insights into possible solutions. Your listening to the students can help them develop trust in a caring adult. As that trust is built, you can work with each child on strategies for coping with grief, fear and anger.

Be sure to allow the students some time each day to write in their journals. If possible, continue the activity throughout the year.

Centering and Balancing
Three Meditations

Objectives:

The students will:

> identify and label stressful situations associated with strong negative emotions.

> experience simple meditation exercises that can be used to relieve stress and regain emotional balance.

Materials:

for the music meditation, a cassette or CD player and a tape or disk of classical or new age relaxation music

Procedure:

Begin this activity by talking with the students about what it means to be out of balance. Start with bodily examples, which the students will relate to immediately, then move the discussion toward emotions. For example, ask: *How many of you have ever lost your balance?*

Ask two or three volunteers to demonstrate what happened when they lost their balance. Establish the concept of a *center* around which weight is distributed evenly when we are *in* balance, and that getting *off* balance usually means that too much weight has shifted to one side or another.

Then, in your own words, explain: *Losing our balance in gymnastics, walking along a wall, riding a bike, or skating are examples that occur on the <u>outside</u>, with our bodies. But we can get out of balance <u>inside</u>, too. One way we can get out of balance inside is from strong negative emotions. If we get very nervous or angry or afraid, we start to feel and act out of control or unbalanced. Can you think of a time when you were out of balance because of negative feelings?*

Invite several students to share experiences in which they felt controlled by negative emotions. List the emotions they mention on the board. Then explain further:

To get back in balance, we have to become centered again. Being centered inside means being quiet, calm, relaxed, and alert. Today, we re going to practice some simple exercises that will help us become centered.

Lead the students in one or more of the following exercises. When you have finished, facilitate a summary discussion using the questions below. Encourage the students to practice centering exercises whenever they feel stressed or out of balance.

Simple Meditation

Tell the students to sit comfortably and close their eyes. Then, slowly read this centering exercise in a soothing tone:

Take several deep breaths . . . Feel your body begin to relax . . . Breathe in and hold it . . . breathe out. . . Breathe in and hold it . . . breathe out. . . Focus your attention on your feet. . . Breathe in so deeply that you can feel the air move through your body . . . all the way to your toes. . . Do that again . . . this time feel the air sweeping all the tension and negative feelings with it . . . Breathe out . . . releasing the tension . . . pushing out the negative feelings. . . Feel your body relax more and more with each breath. . . Feel your stomach relax . . . your heart . . . your chest . . . your shoulders . . . Keep breathing . . . deeply . . . until all of the tension has left your body . . . Then, when you are ready, bring your awareness back to this room and open your eyes.

Visual Meditation

Ask the students to pick out an object somewhere in the room and go sit near it. (It s okay if several students pick the same object, just as long as they can all gather around it without crowding one another.) Explain that the object can be a book, ball, picture, flower, light fixture, etc. When all of the students have picked an object and are settled, say to them:

Focus all of your attention on the object. . . Fix your eyes on it . . . Without looking away, begin to breathe deeply and slowly . . . Slowly and deeply . . . Let your body relax . . . Let your arms relax . . . let your shoulders relax . . . let your legs and feet relax . . . As you look at this object, begin to feel its energy . . . the energy that gives it shape . . . and color . . . the energy that attracted you to it . . . Let yourself connect with the energy in this object . .

(Continued)

33

. Let any tension or negative feelings that you have flow out of you . . . and into this object . . . Keep breathing deeply . . . while you watch the tension leave you . . . and flow in a stream . . .across space . . . and into the object . . . Send all of it there . . . and relax . . . relax . . . relax . . . . When you are completely relaxed, look away from the object and come back to this room.

Music Meditation

Take a cassette or CD of relaxing classical or new age music with you to class. Tell the students to sit comfortably and close their eyes. Begin playing the music at a low volume while you give these directions:

Take several deep breaths . . . and, as you listen to the music . . . begin to relax your body . . . Relax your feet and legs . . . Relax your stomach and back . . . relax your chest . . . relax your arms and shoulders . . . relax your neck . . . and relax all the features of your face . . . . Now, breathe deeply . . . and imagine that you are breathing in the music . . . breathing it into your lungs . . . where it enters your blood . . . carried by millions of molecules of oxygen . . . to all parts of your body . . . Feel the music as it flows through your arms . . . and hands . . . to the tips of your fingers . . . Feel it flow through your heart . . . your stomach . . . into your legs . . . and your feet . . . all the way to your toes . . . Let the music wash away any last bit of tension left in your body . . . Feel it swirl over and around any negative feelings . . . and carry them away . . . Negative feelings have no power against this music . . . They simply disappear . . . . so let them go . . . . and when they are all gone . . . open your eyes . . . and come back to this room.

Discussion Questions:

1. How did you feel when you were doing these relaxation exercises? How did you feel immediately afterwards?
2. Why is it important to stay in balance, or get back in balance when you are stressed?
3. When you feel stressed or upset, what happens to your ability to study and learn?
4. How might you use exercises like this on your own, at school or at home?

The Ups and Downs of Feelings

Experience Sheet and Discussion

Objectives:

The students will:

   identify a number of feelings and link them to specific events in their lives.

   take responsibility for negative feelings by engaging in activities that relieve stress and build positive energy.

Materials:

one copy of the experience sheet, The Roller Coaster Ride of Life for each student; chalkboard and chalk

Procedure:

When you greet the students, ask them how they are. If someone says fine or great, ask: *Does fine mean that you are having a good day? What's causing you to feel good?*

Initiate a discussion about how different events and our thoughts about those events cause us to have various feelings. Give several examples, and elicit others from the group.

Draw a roller-coaster line on the board. Trace the peaks and valleys with your finger (to illustrate) as you introduce the roller-coaster analogy. In your own words, say:

Life is similar to a roller-coaster ride. When good things happen, we go shooting up to the highest points and we feel elated and joyful. When not-so-good things happen, we start coming down again. We may feel uncertain, confused, or unhappy. Certain events take us all the way to the bottom, where we experience grief and anger. When that happens, we have to build up lots of energy in order to climb to the top again.

(Continued)

35

Distribute the experience sheets, and tell the students that you want them to take a few minutes to think about the highs and lows on their own roller-coaster ride. Go over the directions; then give the students about 10 minutes to complete the sheet. While they are working, label the roller coaster on the board with three high events and two low events from your own experience.

When the students have finished, share with them your own events (from the board). Then have them share what they have written in groups of four or five. In a culminating discussion, talk about the need to accept all feelings, whether pleasant or unpleasant. Focus on ways of building or renewing energy during low points.

Discussion Questions:

1. Do you know of any roller coasters with tracks that are flat and even? Do you think such a roller coaster would be fun?
2. Do you think it s possible to never feel sad or angry? Why or why not?
3. How do your thoughts about an event cause you to have certain feelings?
4. If you could control your thoughts, how do you think it would affect your feelings?
5. Why is it important to let off steam when we feel angry or sad?
6. Who is in control of your feelings? ...of your thoughts?

The Roller-Coaster Ride of Life

Experience Sheet

Life sure has ups and downs, doesn t it? Some times your feelings lift you way up, and sometimes they drag you way down. The ride of life is a lot like a roller coaster ride.

It s normal to feel bad when you re down. What are some of your lowest lows? Pick two from the list, or think of others. Then turn the page and write them on the lines below the roller coaster. Write three of your highest highs on the lines at the top of the roller coaster.

HIGHS

When:
 you get a new pet
 you make a new friend
 you take a trip or vacation
 you get an A
 your parents are in a great mood
 someone really listens to you
 you look your best
 you are having fun with friends
 you buy something new
 your team wins
 you feel confident about an assignment or task

LOWS

When:
 your pet is lost or dies
 a friend moves away
 you move away from friends
 you get a bad grade on a test
 your parents argue
 no one seems to understand you
 you think you are unattractive
 there s nothing to do and no one to play with
 you don t have enough money to do something you really want to do
 you lose a game or contest
 you don t feel capable of doing an assignment or task

(Continued)

When you feel low, try not to sit around feeling sorry for yourself. Do something to get rid of those bad feelings. Here are some ideas. **Write two of your favorite activities on the blank lines.**

1. Talk to someone who cares.

2. Go for a bike ride, walk, or jog.

3. Write about your feelings in your diary or journal.

4. Read a book, watch a video, or play a computer game.

5. Play with your pet.

6. Bake a cake or cookies.

7. Draw, paint, sew, sculpt, or design.

8. Pull weeds or fix something that s broken.

9. Listen to music or play an instrument.

10. Rearrange your room.

11. _____

12. _____

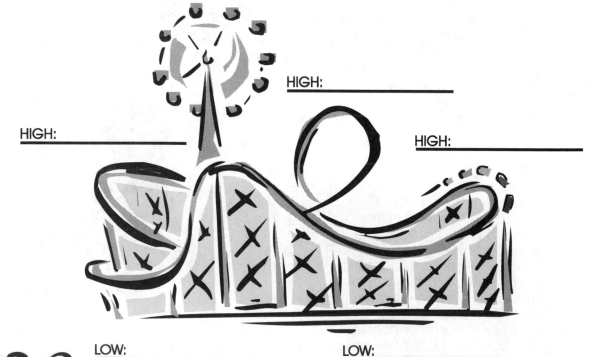

HIGH: _____

HIGH: _____

HIGH: _____

LOW: _____

LOW: _____

Grief Activities

The Land Remembers
Oral Reading and Discussion

Objective:

The students will explore their own feelings about death and renewal.

Materials:

The Land Remembers, Part Six: An Ending, a Beginning, by Ben Logan.

Procedure:

Tell the students you are going to read aloud the last chapter of the book, *The Land Remembers,* which is entitled An Ending, a Beginning. The book tells the story of the adolescent years of a man named Ben Logan. Suggest that the students close their eyes and imagine each scene as they listen.

Discussion Questions:

After you have finished reading the story, ask the students:

1. How did you feel at different points during the story? (As the students call out their responses, list them on the chalkboard.)
2. How was this story an ending and a beginning?
3. Why do you think Ben planted the garden?
4. When did Ben seem to accept his feelings of grief?
5. Why do people cry when they are feeling strong painful emotions like grief?

Discuss the importance of crying as a natural restorative function that helps us to resolve our hurts.

Note: Sometimes an activity of this nature will trigger expressions of grief in students. If crying occurs, demonstrate full acceptance of this natural behavior. Do not urge students to stop crying. Rather, let them know that you appreciate their demonstrations of trust in the class.

THE LAND REMEMBERS
THE STORY OF A FARM AND ITS PEOPLE

PART SIX: AN ENDING, A BEGINNING

by Ben Logan

Mother died the winter I was sixteen. There was no warning. The winter, the same winter that always killed her fall flowers and sent her birds away, caused her death. She fell on the ice and broke her leg. Dr. Farrell came. He growled at her, put a cast on her leg, and told her to rest. Before his horse was out of sight, she was beginning to run the house from her bed. The door to the bedroom stayed open, and her voice carried through the house. Our voices carried back to her, so she felt a part of things.

Two weeks later she woke Father in the night, saying she felt faint. He called Dr. Farrell, but in a few minutes she was dead. The rest of us were still sleeping. Dr. Farrell said a piece of tissue had broken loose from the fracture and stopped her heart.

The weeks crept by. The hushed and whispering feel of death went away, but the house stayed quiet and empty. We would find ourselves wandering from room to room. A thousand times I started out to look for her, to tell her something, to ask her something. In the evening, at the dining-room table, one of us would suddenly raise his head from whatever he was doing and look around, still surprised to find the empty chair at the end of the table nearest the kitchen.

We could not believe she was gone. Even with the constant flow of the seasons to tell us that life is filled with endings and beginnings, there had been no preparation for life on our hilltop world without Mother.

As the winter went on, there were two things I began to dread, the next blizzard and the coming of spring. The blizzard came a month later. I woke in the night, the heavy covers pushing me down, the air in the bedroom cold on my face. Snow was whispering against the walls. The windows were rattling. That odd, deep howling of the wind was coming from the eaves along the west side of the house.

I waited, shivering. The other sound began. The piano was humming, imitating the wind. I listened and waited for the hair to rise on the back of my neck. That didn't happen. It wasn't a lonely, ghostly sound at all. I stopped shivering, pulled the covers up tight around me, and went back to sleep, thinking of her playing and singing at the piano.

The days lengthened. The snow began to melt. Easter lilies bloomed, bright yellow against the brown of last year's grass. The birds came back. The land warmed in the sun, as it had in other springs. The green came again. The silly McMahon tree bloomed on one side.

Nothing had been said about a garden. One Saturday morning at breakfast I asked Lyle to get the ground ready. Everyone stopped eating. We all looked at Father. He put his hands up to his face and didn't speak.

"All right," Lyle said. He smiled, the first one I'd seen from him in a long time. "But don't be surprised if you find a horse's

(Continued)

head sticking in through a window. I might as well as try to plow a postage stamp."

Father got up and started out. He came back and put his hand on my shoulder. "You want any help?"

I shook my head.

Lyle began on the garden, first a load of manure, then the walking plow. I dug through the pantry and found the cardboard box with all the packets of seeds. Mother had written little notes to herself on the envelopes which held seeds we had harvested ourselves. They all made sense but one. It said, "Try a half row, next to the larkspur. Not blue???"

I went out with the box of seeds, the string, and the garden tools just as Lyle was finishing. His face was all puckered up like he wanted to cry. He said something I couldn't understand. He turned his face away and whacked the horses with the lines. They trotted toward the barnyard, the harrow bouncing and clattering behind them.

The garden was smoother than I'd ever seen it. The moist dark soil was already warming in the sun, sending up the fresh smell that said "seedtime." Without thought, I began to follow the pattern of other years. I stretched the string across the garden, lined up with the west window on one side and the wild plum tree on the other, leaving the north end for volunteer ground cherries and tomatoes. I made a row under the string, and began to drop the seeds and cover them with moist earth.

White petals were falling from the McMahon tree. A robin was building its nest again in exactly the same place in the juniper tree. A meadow lark sang from the top of the big maple tree.

I planted radishes, lettuce, turnips, beets, beans, working my way slowly toward the south end. I didn't know yet if I was going to plant any flowers.

The soil went on warming in the sun, beginning to have a lighter color on the very top as it dried out a little. The knees on my trousers were damp. The mysterious living seeds passed through my fingers, one by one. I marked the end of each row with a stick, sometimes putting an empty seed envelope over it so I would know what was there.

I planted the peas, two rows close together, then a space and two more rows, still not knowing why we did it that way.

Finally there was only the space at the south end where the flowers had always been. I looked at it, lying smooth and undisturbed, and knew I couldn't leave it that way. I got the dry and shriveled dahlia roots and gladiolus bulbs from the cellar. Even as I put them carefully into the ground, I couldn't quite believe that life was stored in there, waiting for a chance to come out.

I began on the annual flowers, first the larkspur. Had she liked it so much because of the word "lark" in the name? I had never thought about that. I planted the half row of mystery seeds next to the larkspur, then the zinnias, nasturtiums, and cosmos. Last of all, I sprinkled the tiny black seeds of moss rose and patted them into the ground with a board.

When it was all finished, I straightened up to uncrick my muscles, putting my head way back, looking up at all the different shades of blue. Then, like Lyle, I started crying. I climbed high into the white pine tree, up to my special whorl of limbs. Curled around the trunk the way I'd done when I was younger, with the branches of the big maple tree reaching out toward me, I let go and cried for the first time without trying to stop.

I had not entirely lost her after all. The seeds germinated. Neat rows of new green pushed up in the garden. The land remembers.

What Good Are Feelings?
Experience Sheet

Why do some feelings hurt so much?

Nobody knows the answer to that question for sure. But people have noticed that some *good* can come from painful emotions.

Let s talk about one of the most painful emotions of all   grief.

> When Harold s father died, Harold hurt so badly inside he could hardly stand it. People had told him all his life that men don t cry, but Harold couldn t help it. He didn t care if people thought he was a baby. He cried almost all the time for days, which seemed to Harold to last forever.
> Then one day, Harold woke up feeling different. He was still very sad, and when he thought about his love for his dad, he began to cry again. But the crying was different. It wasn t as deep. And his insides didn t hurt so much anymore.
> After that Harold felt better. He remained sad for a time, but he found that he had truly accepted his father s death. He still loved the memory of his father, and he missed him very much, but his grief had been expressed. He was through crying and ready to go on living.

When people allow themselves to feel grief and express it by crying, they get over the grief faster. People who pretend that they don t feel grief, who hold it inside, stay sad for a very long time. Some people shut their feelings down completely and stay shut down for years   sometimes for the rest of their lives! If people don t express their grief through crying, they may never get over the hurt.

Another painful feeling is guilt. Have you ever done something you felt guilty about afterwards? Guilt makes us feel bad about ourselves, but it can also cause us to make important changes in our behavior. Here s what one person who felt guilty had to say:

(Continued)

43

I took money from another student. She knew I saw where she put it, and she asked me about it. I lied and told her I didn't know a thing about her money.

Afterward I felt rotten inside. The little bit of money I got just wasn't worth it. Stealing and lying made me lose my self-respect. I decided I'd never steal again and I'd try to be more honest. Since I made that decision, I've never stolen again. I've bent the truth, but I haven't told any lies that have caused anybody to get hurt. I feel lots better about myself now.

Take a moment to think about some other feelings. In the spaces below, describe some problems you think these feelings can cause:

Self-pity

_____

_____

_____

Greed

_____

_____

_____

Jealousy

_____

_____

_____

Possessiveness

_____

_____

_____

44

Dealing with Loss
Presentation, Sharing, and Discussion

Objectives:

The students will:

describe a personal loss.

discuss the five stages of dealing with loss.

identify the stage they are presently in and the feelings they are experiencing.

Materials:

chalkboard or chart paper

Procedure:

Begin this activity by introducing students to the topic of loss. For example, you might say:

We experience many kinds of loss in our lives the death of a family member or friend, the loss of a parent through divorce, friends moving away, a pet dying, a relationship breaking up. When something like this happens, our strong feelings can make it very difficult to cope. It helps to know that other people experience losses and get through them. It also helps to understand the stages our feelings go through as we adjust to the loss.

Ask the students to think of a loss they have experienced. Invite them to tell the group:
the nature of the loss (death, divorce, etc.)
when it happened
how they are feeling about it now
any other details they would like to mention

As the students share, model active listening and facilitate discussion.

Next, introduce the five stages of loss first described by Elisabeth Kubler-Ross in her book *On Death and Dying*. As you explain each stage (suggested explanations appear in italics), invite the students to add observations from their own experiences. Taking the time to elicit their contributions will enrich the discussion immensely.

(Continued) 45

Stages of Loss

¥ Denial

When you know you are about to lose someone or something that you value, the first reaction is disbelief. No, this can t be happening. Everything will be okay tomorrow. This is just a bad dream. I ll wake up soon.

¥ Anger

When you can no longer deny the loss, you experience frustration and anger. What did I do to deserve this? How can s/he do that to me? This could only happen in an unfair, stupid world.

¥ Bargaining

After you express your anger, you may begin to feel hopeful again. You think, Maybe if I m a better person, Dad will stay. If I promise to help take care of her, maybe God will let Grandma live. I ll change all of my bad habits and she ll like me again.

¥ Grieving

At this stage, you allow yourself to feel the pain and hurt. You may cry a lot and feel very depressed and hopeless. Difficult as it is, this is a very important stage. A person can t fully recover from a loss without grieving.

¥ Acceptance

Finally, you start to feel okay again. You may still be sad sometimes, but life returns to normal and you no longer think constantly about the person or condition you lost.

Point out that people don t always go through the stages in sequence. Sometimes they bounce back and forth between a couple of stages for a long time. In some cases, completing the cycle can take many months. Friends, relatives, and teachers who don t realize how long it can take may wonder why the person hasn t snapped out of it.

Use the remainder of the time to facilitate discussion concerning the stages.

Discussion Questions:

1. How many of the stages have you been through?
2. How did you feel at each stage and how did you behave?
3. Which of the five stages are you in right now?
4. Many people who want to help simply don t know what to do or say. What would you like them to do or say?
5. What have you learned from this activity?

A Letter to...
Guided Imagery, Writing and Discussion

Objectives:

The students will:

recall a happy memory involving a person they have lost.

express their feelings and thoughts by writing a letter to the person.

Materials:

writing paper; cassette tape or CD player and relaxing music (optional)

Procedure:

Have the students close their eyes and take a comfortable position. If you have music, begin to play it at a low volume. In a gentle but audible voice, read the following guided imagery exercise, pausing for at least 5 seconds between phrases.

Take a deep breath and let it out slowly . . . Begin to relax your body and your mind . . . Keep breathing deeply . . . Feel the tension leave each part of your body . . . Relax your feet and ankles . . . you calves and thighs . . . your hips, stomach, and chest . . . your hands and arms. . . your back, shoulders and neck . . . your face . . . And while you are relaxing, begin to think about the person you have lost . . . See the person exactly the way you like to remember him or her . . . Picture everything in detail . . . And with this image in your mind, begin to recall a happy memory that you shared with the person . . . a vacation, a job that you did together, a meal . . . Remember it in detail . . . Recall the surroundings . . . the sounds . . . the aromas . . . what you both were wearing . . . what you said . . . how you felt . . . Keep breathing deeply while you relive completely that happy memory (pause 15 seconds) . . . Now, think of something that you would like to say to the person you lost . . . If you could communicate with this person right now, what would your message be? . . . Would you tell the person what you appreciated about him or her? . . . Would you share the memory you just recalled? . . . Would you ask a question? . . . See yourself speaking to the person now (pause 15 seconds) . . . When you are finished, say good-by to the person . . . Take your time . . . Know that you can revisit this person in your mind whenever you wish . . . When you are

(Continued)

47

ready, open your eyes and return to the group.

Give the students a few moments to readjust, quietly accepting any tears or other expressions of sadness.

Distribute the writing paper. Tell the students that you would like them to write down some of the thoughts and feelings they just experienced in the form of a letter to the person they lost. In your own words, explain:

You don t need to show this letter to anyone, so say whatever you want to say. Perhaps you ll want to write down the same words you said to the person in your imagination, or maybe you want to say something entirely different. It s up to you. Begin your letter with Dear... and the name with which you always addressed the person. Then, simply write. You ll have 15 minutes to complete your letter.

When the students have finished writing, you may wish to facilitate a culminating discussion.

Discussion Questions:

1. How has your life changed since you lost this person?
2. What is hardest about dealing with the loss right now?
3. What did you learn from the things we did here today?

Crises Happen
An Art Activity with Discussion

Objectives:

The students will:

utilize artistic expression to capture feelings and thoughts related to a personal crisis.

learn ways of better coping with crisis situations.

Materials:

drawing paper, colored markers and/or crayons, and other art materials; chalkboard and chalk

Procedure:

Ask the students if they know what the word *crisis* means. Listen to and reflect the students responses. Explain that a crisis is a time when a big change occurs in a person s life, often caused by a loss of some kind, and always accompanied by strong emotions. Give several examples of personal crisis events and ask the students to think of others. Write them on the chalkboard. Your list should include:

death of a relative
death of a friend or pet
parents divorce or separation
parent s loss of a job
moving and leaving friends
family illness or accident
being hurt or abused

Distribute the art materials and ask the students to draw a picture of a personal crisis that they have experienced. Allow at least 15 minutes for this process. Then ask volunteers to share their drawing with the class, explaining details of the event and how they felt.

Facilitate discussion after each sharing. Talk in general about thoughts and feelings that people typically experience in connection with the type of crisis shared. In the process, make these points:
¥ Every crisis eventually passes.

(Continued)

¥ Painful, hurt feelings are gradually replaced by more positive feelings.
¥ Family events, such as divorce, are never the child s fault.
¥ There are people in the community who want to help.

Discussion Questions:

1. What kinds of thoughts did you have during your crisis?
2. Which thoughts were helpful? ...not helpful?
3. What feelings did most of us experience at times of crisis?
4. To whom can you go for help during a crisis?
5. What can you do to help yourself?
6. Why do we have a tendency to feel guilty when we lose a person or a pet we love?

Variations:

In a second phase of the activity, allow students who have experienced similar crises to meet in small groups for sharing and further discussion. Suggest that they respond to the topic, How I Survived a Crisis.

Instead of drawing, older students may prefer to write fictionalized accounts of their crises in the form of short stories or plays. After the stories/plays have been written, facilitate peer critiquing sessions, editing, and rewriting. Allow students who wish to share their finished work. Those who write plays should be given an opportunity to cast, rehearse and present them.

That s Unfair!
Neutralizing Resentment

Objectives:

The students will:

> brainstorm enjoyable aspects of their lives.

> develop a personal poster showing the unfair advantages in their lives.

> practice acknowledging unfair advantages as a way of reducing pain and resentment.

Materials:

9" x 12" drawing paper (2 pieces per child); colored pencils, markers or crayons; tape; chalkboard and chalk

Procedure:

Begin by gathering the students together and asking them to brainstorm a list describing enjoyable aspects of their lives. Allow the students to contribute anything that they consider an advantage.   Suggest that they think of situations, conditions or things that other kids in the world may not have the opportunity to enjoy, such as the positive features of their home, school, neighborhood, community, and country. Write all their responses on the board. Consider the following items when making the list; however, *include only those that are real for your students.*

> having a TV or VCR
> having caring parents
> being able to play video games
> owning a bike
> living in an area where there s snow (ocean, mountains, etc.)
> being allowed to play in Little League
> being able to participate in Scouts or other clubs
> having nice grandparents
> having a nice place to live (apartment, house)
> having a warm, comfortable bed to sleep in
> being healthy
> being able to eat yummy foods like pizza, burgers, apples, popcorn, tortilla chips, etc.

(Continued)

having sufficient food to eat
having parents who are not abusive (alcoholics, criminals)
having a computer (at home or school)
being able to talk to friends on the phone
being able to get a free education
living in a country where people can voice their opinions
living in a country where people can vote for their officials

After their ideas have been exhausted, ask the students to look at the advantages that apply to them personally. In your own words, tell them: *Having all these advantages (and more) is really unfair! In some countries the children are dying of starvation and have never attended a school or visited a doctor. Some people have never seen a telephone or radio, let alone a TV or VCR. It is unfair for you to have these things while others go without them!*

Explain that the reason you asked the students to make the list was to demonstrate that some of life s unfairness is positive. When life and/or specific events in life seem unfair, the students can help themselves by thinking of the (unfair) advantages they have. Assure the students that you do not wish to negate their hurts or discount their problems; however, you do want to show them how to ease their pain by focusing on advantages. Suggest that one way of reminding themselves of the advantages they have in life is to illustrate them in a personal poster.

Explain that you want the students to each select 12 advantages to illustrate in a personal poster. When completed, the poster can be displayed on the wall of a bedroom or folded and kept in a notebook, giving the students something to look at when life is unfair and they need a positive boost.

Distribute two sheets of drawing paper to each student. Ask the students to divide each sheet into six equal parts by folding the long side into thirds and the short side in half. The two sheets can be attached with tape along either their short or long edges after the illustrations are finished. Ask the students to illustrate one positive aspect of their life in each of the 12 spaces. Suggest that they give their poster a title, such as My Unfair Advantages, or The Darling Dozen.

To summarize, repeat the idea that there exist as many positive unfairnesses as negative. When the students experience the unfair side of life, they don t always have to choose anger and resentment as a response. They can take a look at their personal poster and be reminded that they benefit from many of life s unfair advantages as well. Remind the students to balance their negative feelings by looking at their posters throughout the year.

Developing Responsible Feelings
Class Discussion and Experience Sheet

Objectives:

The students will:

state that feelings don t just happen, they are chosen.

explain that feelings result from a person s thoughts about a situation, rather than the situation itself.

Materials:

one copy of the experience sheet, Take Responsibility for Your Feelings! for each student

Procedure:

Read the following scenarios to the students. After each scenario, ask the questions provided and encourage discussion about what actually caused the feelings of the individuals involved.

Scenario #1:
Juanita is late for Betty s party. When she arrives at the party, Betty yells at Juanita for not arriving on time. Juanita feels that she s irresponsible and a bad friend.

Discussion Questions:

1. What thoughts do you think Juanita was having after Betty yelled at her?
2. What caused Juanita to feel the way she did?
3. What other thoughts could Juanita have chosen in response to Betty s anger?

(Continued)

Scenario #2

Jim and Bill both try out for quarterback of the school team. In the final round, Jim is selected. Bill feels inferior and rejected.

Discussion Questions:

1. What is inaccurate about Bill s thinking?
2. What else could Bill think about the situation and how would he feel about himself as a result?
3. In general, what causes people to feel the way they do, the situation or the thoughts they have about the situation? Explain your answer.

When you have completed the discussion, distribute the experience sheets and ask the students to complete them. After the students have finished writing, ask volunteers to share their situations and ideas concerning how they can change their thoughts.

Take Responsibility for Your Feelings!

Experience Sheet

We all have situations and conditions in our lives that we feel negatively about. Think about a situation or condition in your life right now (or in the past) that causes you to feel *anger, disappointment, embarrassment, sadness,* or some other negative feeling. Write about the situation here. Describe what is going on and how you feel about it.

_____

_____

_____

_____

_____

_____

Now, take responsibility for your thoughts by changing them. What other thoughts could you have about this situation that would help you to feel better? Be understanding and compassionate with yourself, but be honest, too. (If you need more room, use the back of this sheet.)

_____

_____

_____

_____

_____

_____

55

Fear Activities

Positive vs. Negative
A Cooperative Game

Objectives:

The students will:

> identify fears and worries associated with specific topics.

> make decisions about how to cope with fears and worries.

Materials:

chalkboard and chalk or chart paper and felt-tip marker

Procedure:

List the following topics on the board or chart paper:

- ¥ You are about to take an important test in your worst subject.
- ¥ Tomorrow is your first day in a new school.
- ¥ You are about to try out for the lead in the school play.
- ¥ You have to give a speech to a group of kids you don t know.
- ¥ Your family has moved to another state and you re about to see your new home for the first time.
- ¥ You are home alone at night and you hear a strange noise.

Next, divide the class into two teams and select two students to be judges (along with you). Name the teams the Negative Thinkers and the Positive Thinkers.   Explain that the task of the Negative Thinkers is to suggest things that might be scary, cause worry, or go wrong with each of the scenarios listed on the board. The task of the Positive Thinkers is to offer solutions to the problems suggested by the negative team. If the problem is one that has no solution, the positive thinkers must tell how to make the best of it. Encourage collaboration on both teams.

Begin the game by having the negative team make a suggestion about what might go wrong with the first scenario. Then have the positive team provide a suggestion on how to solve the suggested problem. If the positive team makes a reasonable suggestion (as determined by the three judges) it gets a point. If not, the negative team gets a point. Give all team members an opportunity to suggest a problem or a solution before going on to the next scenario. Have the teams switch roles for the last three scenarios so that both teams have an opportunity to think in both positive and negative terms.

When the game is finished, encourage the students to talk about what they have learned about positive and negative thinking.

One of the Scariest Things That Ever Happened to Me

Story Writing and Role Playing

Objectives:

The students will:

express and share anxieties and fears they have experienced.

explore alternative means of coping with fears.

Materials:

writing materials

Procedure:

Tell the students that you would like them to write down in detail one of the scariest things that ever happened to them. Give a couple of personal examples about scary things that happened to you or to someone you know. As a pre-writing activity, ask volunteers to tell the class about a scary experience they had. Have the students entitle their story, One of the Scariest Things That Ever Happened to Me.

On a following day, have the students read their stories to the class. Allow enough time for everyone to share. Ask questions to obtain additional details.

Divide the class into groups of six to eight. Have each group select a story written by one of its members to role play. After the stories have been selected, have each group fictionalize the account. Write the following steps on the board and have the students follow them:

1. Make up names for the characters.
2. Describe what the characters look like, their ages, how they talk, and any other important descriptive information.
3. Decide from what point of view the story will be told.

4. Describe the setting in detail.

5. Explore plot alternatives and embellish the story.

6. Explore different resolutions to the problem and choose the best solution to role play.

Provide time for each group to plan and rehearse its role play and then allow each group to perform for the rest of the class. Enjoy, and applaud after each dramatization.

Discussion Questions:

After all the role plays have been performed, facilitate a discussion about fear by asking these and other questions:

1. Do you think that sometimes a fear can be caused more by our perception of an event/thing than by the event/thing itself? Explain.

2. How did it feel to talk about a scary experience?

3. What similarities did you notice about the scary things we shared? What differences?

4. What are some things we can do to overcome fears?

5. Why does it help to talk about things we are scared of?

We All Have Fears
Experience Sheet

All people have fears of one type or another. Some people are afraid of high places, others of being embarrassed. Some are afraid of death or the dark.

Below is a list of things that often scare people. Look at each item in the left-hand column and circle the number that best describes how you feel.

1 = not afraid.
2 = somewhat afraid
3 = afraid
4 = very afraid
5 = extremely afraid

In the right-hand column, write a suggestion to yourself about what you can do to be less afraid.

How afraid am I?	Things I can do to be less afraid
1 2 3 4 5 afraid of the dark	
1 2 3 4 5 afraid of speaking in front of a group	
1 2 3 4 5 afraid of being alone	
1 2 3 4 5 afraid of strangers	
1 2 3 4 5 afraid of getting poor grades	
1 2 3 4 5 afraid of high places	
1 2 3 4 5 afraid of the dentist	

How afraid am I?	Things I can do to be less afraid

1 2 3 4 5   afraid of doing
something wrong   _____

1 2 3 4 5   afraid of parents
getting divorced   _____

1 2 3 4 5   afraid of horror movies _____

1 2 3 4 5   afraid of being
laughed at   _____

1 2 3 4 5   afraid of being
beaten up   _____

1 2 3 4 5   afraid of fire   _____

1 2 3 4 5   afraid of being
yelled at   _____

1 2 3 4 5   afraid of being hurt   _____

1 2 3 4 5   afraid of big dogs   _____

63

Rational Fears vs. Irrational Fears

Class Discussion

Objectives:

The students will:

verbalize some of their fears.

distinguish between rational and irrational fears.

Materials:

writing materials for each student; chalkboard and chalk; one copy of the experience sheet, Fear Is a Monster, for each student

Procedure:

Ask the students to take a few moments to think about some fears they have. Explain that fear is an emotion that causes distress, anxiety, or a sense of dread, and that everyone is afraid of something. As an example, tell the students about one or two things that you are afraid of. Next, ask the students to write down four or five of their fears. After everyone has finished, ask volunteers to share some of their fears. Be accepting of all contributions and don t allow any put-downs or laughing as the students share.

Explain to the students that people are wise to have some fears, because they serve as protection from harm. Fears of driving too fast and taking illegal drugs are examples of rational fears. However, some fears are irrational   they provide no self-protection and serve no useful purpose. In fact, these fears sometimes keep people from enjoying life fully and from doing things they would otherwise like to do. Fears of the dark and flying are examples of irrational fears.

Make two columns on the board with the headings, Rational Fears and Irrational Fears. Collect the students papers and, without indicating who s paper you are reading, call out different fears. As you read each fear, have the students decide if it is rational or irrational. Record the fear in the appropriate column.

Ask for suggestions on how to deal with some of the irrational fears listed. Next, pass out the experience sheet, Fear Is a Monster, and give the students a few minutes to complete it.

Discussion Questions:

As a conclusion, ask these and other questions:

1. How did it feel to talk about a fear?
2. How do you feel now after sharing the fear?
3. What have you learned about yourself from thinking about or sharing fears?
4. What steps can we take to overcome fears?

65

Fear Is a Monster

Experience Sheet

Think about times when you were afraid of some-one or something, but everything turned out okay. Just as monsters aren t real, most of the time our fears aren t real either. Think of it this way:

FEAR = False Evidence Appearing Real

In the left-hand column, write about irrational fears you have had. In the right-hand column, describe what really happened.

My fear   **What really happened**

_____   _____

_____   _____

_____   _____

_____   _____

_____   _____

_____   _____

_____   _____

Good Tips!

Here are some things you can do to get over irrational fears:
1. Admit the fear to yourself.
2. Tell a trusted adult about your fear.
3. Keep a journal. Write about events or things that cause you fear.
4. Talk with your teacher or guidance counselor.

Writing in your journal, or sharing your fears with others can often help you get over irrational fears. But remember, changing your feelings takes time and patience.

Fear Busters
Class Discussion and Cooperative Activity

Objectives:

The students will:
> identify specific irrational fears.
> describe steps for overcoming irrational fears.

Materials:

chalk and chalkboard; writing materials

Procedure:

Begin this activity by reminding the students that everyone has fears, but that some fears are irrational   they are built around things that pose no real threat. Sometimes fears can become a very serious problem to individuals. These extreme fears are called *phobias*. People with a serious phobia often have a problem enjoying life to the fullest because their fear keeps them from doing certain things. Mention several phobias like: *claustrophobia* fear of small/closed places,   *acrophobia* - fear of high places, etc., and explain how these phobias negatively affect people s lives. Explain that phobias like this can often be prevented if people face, understand, and use strategies to overcome their fears.

Next, ask the students to call out fears that they or others have. Write these fears on the board. After a number of fears have been listed, ask the students to form groups of four. Assign one fear to each group, and tell the groups that they are now Fear Busters. Their job is to discuss the best way to overcome their assigned fear. Explain that you want the groups to take 10 minutes to brainstorm as many ideas as they can think of. (Remind the students that there are no bad ideas, and that all suggestions are accepted during a brainstorming session.) Have the groups record all ideas.

Finally, have the groups take another 10 minutes to go over all ideas and select the one or two methods that have the best chance of overcoming

(Continued)

their assigned fear. At the end of the second 10 minutes, ask each group to report to the rest of the class. When all groups have shared, lead a culminating discussion.

Discussion Questions:

1. What have you learned about fears from this activity?
2. Do you think there are things you can do in your life right now to overcome fear? What are they?
3. What is the meaning of the quotation, There is nothing to fear but fear itself ?

Variation:

Have the groups create and dramatize skits or role plays that demnstrate their assigned fear and the methods for overcoming it.

Scary Stories
Story-Writing and Discussion

Objectives:

The students will:

> express current or past anxieties and fears and explore alternative methods of coping with them.

> write stories based on real experiences.

Materials:

writing materials for the students

Procedure:

If possible, have the students sit in a single large circle. Introduce the activity by acknowledging matter-of-factly that everyone is afraid sometimes. Then ask the students to think of something they are afraid of, and invite several students to tell the group what they fear. Choose one of the contributions, and suggest that the students create a group story about it. Go around the circle and have each child in turn add a sentence to the story. For example, if one of the students says, I m afraid of big dogs, the story might begin something like this:

You: *I m walking home and I see a big dog.*
First child: *The dog starts to bark at me.*
Second child: *I m afraid the dog will bite me.*
Third child: *I cross to the other side of the street.*
Fourth child: *The dog comes after me.*
Etc.

When you have finished going around the circle, facilitate a discussion about the fear expressed and the strategies that the students came up with, as part of their story, for dealing with the fear. Ask what other strategies might have been used, and discuss alternatives. If the story becomes outlandish, point out the need for legitimate caution (toward, for example, strange animals) and contrast probable and improbable events, as well as reasonable and unreasonable fears.

(Continued)

Next, write several story-starters on the board. For example:
The scariest thing that ever happened to me was...
The most frightening place I ever visited was...
Once I got very afraid when...
Sometimes I feel scared because...

Have the students return to their regular seats. Distribute the writing materials. Working individually, have the students select a story starter and use it to begin the first sentence of a short story. In your own words, elaborate:

Write a one-page story about your scary event. Tell who else was involved, what you did in response to your fear, and how the situation turned out.

Allow about 15 minutes for writing. Then, as time permits, invite volunteers to read their stories to the class. Use each story to stimulate discussion about fear and various alternatives for responding to fear. Ask some of the questions below.

Discussion Questions:

1. Why do people feel afraid? What good does it do?
2. What kinds of things did most of us seem to be afraid of?
3. How often do the things we fear turn out to be harmless?
4. When feelings of fear are making it hard for you to work, play or eat, what can you do about it?
5. When you feel afraid, whom can you talk to at home? ...at school?

On the Fear Line
Discriminating Between Rational and Irrational Fears

Objectives:

The students will:

publicly acknowledge that they do have fears

understand the difference between rational and irrational fears

consider alternative ways of handling a variety of fears.

Materials:

chalkboard and chalk; scratch paper

Procedure:

Announce that the subject of today s discussion is fear. Ask for a show of hands from students who have *never* felt afraid. If you get any hands at all, merely take note and then ask how many have felt afraid of something. Most hands will go up.

Acknowledge that it takes courage to talk about our fears, and you appreciate the willingness of students to participate.

Draw a long horizontal line on the chalkboard. At one end, draw a determined looking face and label it Fearless Fairburn. At the other end draw a frightened looking face and label it Frightened Finlay. Explain to the students that Fairburn and Finlay are at the very extreme ends of the fear line, which means they are completely opposite each other when it comes to being afraid.

Enlist the students help in describing Fairburn and Finlay. For example:

Fearless Fairburn eats raw meat, rides a bike down the center line with no hands, refuses to wear a seat belt, teases mean-looking dogs, and thinks it would be fun to organize a relay team to race across highways. Frightened Finlay wears a muffler in July, trembles at the sight of a kitten, figures a cut on the finger means the end is near, and won t walk to the mailbox without a companion.

(Continued)

Ask the students to decide where on the line they d place themselves compared to Fairburn and Finlay. Have volunteers come up and write their names (or draw themselves) on the line. Ask each volunteer to tell the group what led him/her to choose that spot on the line. When you run out of volunteers (or when the board gets overly crowded with names), pick the person nearest the center of the line and ask:

How many are more afraid than (name of student)?
How many are less afraid than (name of same student)?

Talk with the group about the difference between rational and irrational (realistic and unrealistic) fears. Point out that rational fears, such as fear of speeding cars, serve a useful purpose. They make us defensive pedestrians and bike riders. On the other hand, a fear of all cars is irrational, because it serves no useful purpose and interferes with leading a normal life.

Next, distribute the scratch paper and ask the students to each write down two fears. Tell them not to put their names on the paper and not to tell anyone what they ve written. Collect the papers.

Have the students form small groups of four or five. Shuffle the papers and divide them up among the groups. Then, in your own words, explain to the students:

Pretend that you are a committee of fear experts, and are meeting to look at some cases. Read each fear and discuss it. Decide first if you think the fear is rational or irrational, and then discuss ways of coping with or overcoming the fear. Write down your thoughts and conclusions on each slip of paper.

Allow the groups about 15 minutes to meet. Circulate and assist, as necessary. Then ask the groups to share their thoughts and conclusions with the class. Lead a culminating discussion.

Discussion Questions:

1. Were most of our fears rational or irrational?
2. How do we learn to be afraid of something?
3. What are some things that you used to be afraid of but no longer fear?
4. What did you learn that helped you outgrow your fear?
5. What new ideas did you get today for coping with a fear?

Anger Activities

Sequencing Anger
Moderating Thoughts to Reduce Anger

Objectives:

The students will:

demonstrate an understanding of an anger sequence: event-thoughts-feelings.

practice substituting moderate thoughts for angry thoughts as one way of reducing anger.

Materials:

chalkboard and chalk, writing paper, pencils

Procedure:

Tell the students that in this activity they will have an opportunity to discover a new way of handling anger. Ask them to consider that angry feelings are not actually caused by situations and events, but rather by the *thoughts* one has about those situations and events. Once the thoughts about an event (often extreme) are identified, those thoughts can be replaced with different thoughts (usually more moderate) as one way of controlling anger. Explain to the students that you are going to demonstrate this concept using a chart on the board.

Write four headings across the top of the board: **Event, Thoughts, Feelings,** and **Substitute Thoughts.** Under the **Event** column write *Mom won t let me go to the dance with my friends*. Skip the second column and ask the students what their feelings might be in this situation. The students will probably suggest words such as mad, furious, and miserable. Write several of these words in the **Feelings** column. Then go back to the **Thoughts** column, and ask the students what their thoughts might be concerning the same situation. Elicit answers such as these: *She s being mean. She doesn t understand how important it is to me. She never wants me to have fun.*

Explain to the students that it is not the event, but the *thoughts* about the event that cause the feelings. Refer to the sentences in the second column and point out that any of these thoughts about the event could create angry feelings. Explain that no situation, event, or person *makes* us have a particular feeling. Through our thoughts, we *choose* our feelings, even if we are not aware of it.

Next, suggest that if the thoughts recorded in the second column can be moderated, the feelings too will change. Help the students create new thought statements such as: *Mom thinks she is looking out for my safety. She has family plans the night of the dance and wants me to be with the family. There will be more dances this year.* Record them in the last column, **Substitute Thoughts**. Point out that these moderated thoughts will reduce the anger.

Distribute writing paper and pencils. Ask the students to divide their paper in half lengthwise creating two columns. Have them write the heading *Event* at the top of the left-hand column and the heading *Thoughts* at the top of the right-hand column. Next, instruct the students to turn their paper over and create two more columns. Direct them to write the headings *Feelings* and *Substitute Thoughts* above the left and right columns on this side.

Under the first heading, ask the students to list three real or hypothetical situations/events in which they are certain they would feel angry. In the second column (adjacent to each description), have them write the thoughts they would have in each situation. On the other side of the paper, ask them to write down the feelings that these thoughts would create. Finally, challenge the students to come up with moderated thoughts that could be substituted for the original thoughts about the situation.

When all of the students have completed their charts, invite individuals to share one or more of their anger sequences. After each example, ask the group how their feelings might change as a result of the substitute thoughts. Emphasize that when they find themselves reacting to a situation too strongly, the students can improve their disposition by rethinking the situation. This ability takes practice and perseverance, but it works!

Discussion Questions:

To summarize, ask the students to think about and/or respond to the following questions:

1. Why do we choose to feel angry in certain situations?
2. When you are angry, why is it important to rethink the situation?
3. What is easy about sequencing anger? What is difficult about it?

Personal Anger Scale
Experience Sheet

Becoming aware of how angry you feel in certain situations can help you deal with the feelings, manage your behaviors, and solve or cope with the problem. Below are some circumstances that may or may not make you angry.

Using the scale, rank your anger in each situation.

       1-no big deal 2-somewhat annoyed 3-upset 4-angry 5-furious

___   You are walking on the school grounds when someone calls you a name that puts down your religious or ethnic heritage.

___   You are in a meeting or doing group work. One person is dominating the conversation and bossing everyone around.

___   Someone keeps telling you what to do when you already know what to do.

___   Someone yells comments to you about being overweight or underweight.

___   Everyone is talking in class but you get singled out and scolded for your behavior.

___   Someone copies your book report and turns it in as his/her own.

___   Someone makes fun of one of your family members or friends.

___   After working hard at school and team practice, you get yelled at by your parents for work you haven t finished at home.

___   Your best friend invites someone else to go with him/her to Disneyland.

___   You are in a store and the clerk keeps waiting on adults instead of you.

═══ NOW DO THIS ═══

On the back of this sheet write about something that *really* happened to you that made you angry.

76

Let s Make Up
Writing a Letter to Make It Better

Objectives:

The students will:

> practice writing a letter to someone at whom they were once angry.

> identify letter-writing as one way to deal with anger and/or resolve a conflict.

Materials:

one copy per student of the worksheet, Make It Better Letter, and pencils

Procedure:

Introduce the activity by pointing out that friends and family members sometimes have misunderstandings and conflicts. When they do, all parties experience some kind of anger, and often someone has to apologize before feelings are soothed.

Explain that, in this activity, the students will learn to write a letter using a form which can help them express their feelings, thoughts, and desires. It is a letter in which no one is blamed or humiliated. Honest feelings are expressed in a non-threatening way. The students can use this letter as a pattern to follow when they experience a conflict with another person and feelings are so strong that the parties cannot face or speak to each other.

Distribute the experience sheets, Make It Better Letter.   Ask the students to think of a time when they were really mad at another person so mad that they couldn t speak to the person. If the students don t remember such an incident, ask that they make up a life-like situation in which they are in conflict with another person. Help the students recall the details of their situation by suggesting that they think about what happened, who was involved, what their first feelings were, why they were angry, and what they wanted.

(Continued)

Guide the students through parts of the letter. Ask that they fill in a real or fictitious name in the greeting.

- ¥ In the first sentence, have the students write down what they were angry about.

- ¥ In the second sentence, have them write down any initial feelings they felt before becoming angry. (See First Feelings activity.)

- ¥ The third sentence tells what the student was thinking in the situation that produced the anger. (See Sequencing Anger activity).

- ¥ Sentence four describes a fear the student had about what happened or might happen.

- ¥ In the fifth sentence, the students write what they are truly sorry about. Emphasize that they are not necessarily making an apology. They are simply explaining why they feel sorry.

- ¥ The sixth sentence expresses a wish or desire.

- ¥ The last two sentences are acknowledgments of the other person. They convey what the writer appreciates in that person and what the other person means to the writer.

After the students have completed their letters, suggest that they use them as a pattern for a letter that they can use in real situations to deal with anger and/or resolve conflict. Explain that the letter need not be sent to the other person. It is mainly a way to clarify the writer s thoughts and feelings and reduce anger and stress.

Make It Better Letter
Experience Sheet

Use this model to write a letter to someone with whom you are angry. Writing this type of letter will help you to clarify your thoughts and feelings. It will also help you reduce anger and stress   even if you never send the letter.

Dear_____,

I m very angry that...

What happened made me think that...

I am (was) afraid that...

I am sorry that...

All I really want(ed) is (was)...

I appreciate...

Thank you for...

Sincerely,

_____

79

First Feelings
Looking at Anger as a Secondary Emotion

Objectives:

The students will:

identify feelings that typically precede/precipitate anger and identify ways to deal with these feelings.

practice acceptable ways to express first feelings.

Materials:

chalkboard and chalk; one copy of the sheet, Dealing with Anger for each student

Procedure:

Introduce this activity by explaining that anger is a normal emotion, experienced by everyone. However, anger tends to be a *secondary* emotion. In other words, one or more *other* feelings usually precede anger. Give the students an example, such as: *You forget to study for a test and fail it. Because the test covered a subject in which you usually do well, you feel disappointed and frustrated. However, those first feelings quickly turn to anger. Before you know it, anger is the only feeling that you are aware of and the only one other people observe in you.*

Continue by introducing a second and related concept: Other people usually have difficulty coping with our anger. If our behavior becomes volatile and aggressive when we are angry, we cause others to feel threatened and maybe even to get angry in return. Other people have an easier time responding to our initial feeling of disappointment, frustration, embarrassment, grief, or fear. Consequently, a valuable skill to develop is the skill of identifying and expressing our initial feelings, rather than just our anger.

Brainstorm some initial emotions that often precede anger and write them on the board. They can include feelings such as sadness, grief, frustration, embarrassment, relief, shock, disappointment, and confusion. Then ask the students to suggest acceptable ways of expressing these feelings that others can identify with.

Distribute the experience sheet, Dealing with Anger. Explain to the students that they will read several scenarios in which anger is preceded by other emotions. Their task is to identify the other emotions and suggest ways in which they can be appropriately expressed. Read and discuss the first scenario together as guided practice. If you feel that the students have a good understanding of the concepts, allow them to do the rest of the experience sheet individually, in pairs, or in small groups.

Discussion Questions:

When the students have finished the sheet, gather the whole group together to discuss the other scenarios. Summarize this activity with a few thinking questions such as these:

1. How does anger mask what is really going on inside someone?
2. Why is anger so difficult to deal with in other people?
3. What are some initial feelings that often precede anger?
4. What are some ways in which we can express our first feelings?

Dealing with Anger
Experience Sheet

Read the following scenarios carefully and answer the questions.

Scenario 1:

Maria was one of the best players on the hockey team. She really wanted to be captain the coming semester and had more than just a good chance of being elected. Her teammates liked and respected her and she got along well with her coach. Maria knew that her grades had to stay above C and she struggled to keep her Social Studies grade up. Poor reading skills kept her from doing very well. When she took her final Social Studies test before semester s end, she thought she had done OK. When report cards came out, however, she saw a D in Social Studies. During hockey practice after school, Maria announced that she didn t want to be captain of the team. When her friends asked her why she had changed her mind, Maria snapped at them and said, Who wants to be captain of this stupid team, anyway? I have better things to worry about than keeping you all in line.

Questions:

What were Maria s initial feelings?

How did she express these feelings?

How could Maria have better expressed her emotions?

Scenario 2:

Nate came to school ready for a fight. The night before, his cat Blackie was run over by a car and killed. Nate's friend, James, greeted him with a friendly punch, What's up, Dude? Nate didn't respond. He just bit his lip. James punched him a little harder and said, What's the matter? You too good for me today? At that, Nate went ballistic and started screaming at James, Can't you keep your hands to yourself? You think you own the place!

Questions:

What were Nate's first feelings before he lost his temper?

How did he express his emotions?

How could he have expressed his first feelings?

Scenario 3:

Marianne went with her class to a 5-day outdoor education camp. She had never been away from home before. The first night, the counselor said that she would tell the girls a ghost story after they were all in their bunks. Marianne started shaking. I hate ghost stories. They're dumb, she protested before the story began. All the other girls called out that they wanted to hear the story. As the counselor began talking, Marianne kept interrupting with comments like This is so stupid, Can I go to the bathroom? and Why do I have to listen to this? Then she began coughing so loudly that the counselor had to stop the story.

Questions:

What were Marianne's first feelings, before she started objecting to the story?

How did she express her emotions?

How could she have better expressed these feelings?

83

What s Your Bag of Tricks?
Anger Control Strategies

Objectives:

The students will:

brainstorm strategies for controlling anger.

field test three to five anger-control strategies over a given period of time.

report back to the group concerning the effectiveness of the selected strategies.

Materials:

chalk and chalkboard; 3" x 5" cards; pencils

Procedure:

Lead a group discussion on what happens when people lose their tempers. Talk about the destructiveness of volatile behaviors and how lack of self-control can increase stress and make a conflict or problem worse. Allow the students to share examples of what happens when someone loses self-control.

Explain to the students that effective solutions to conflicts and problems often require communication, negotiations with others, and long-term effort. However, it is sometimes necessary to gain control of ourselves before attempting such strategies. Instead of throwing tantrums and venting anger in other destructive ways, we can use anger control strategies to put a band aid on a bad situation until we have calmed down enough to work on positive solutions to the problem.

On the chalkboard, write the heading, **Anger Control Strategies**.   Ask the students to brainstorm positive ways in which they can regain self-control when they feel themselves getting angry. Write their ideas on the board as they are suggested. The following items may be included as anger control strategies:

- ¥ Run laps around the house (block, school, track).
- ¥ Leave the situation and take ten slow, deep breaths.
- ¥ Jump on a trampoline or tumbling mat, or with a jump rope.
- ¥ Punch a pillow, mattress, or punching bag.
- ¥ Look away and/or walk away from the cause of stress.
- ¥ Go get a drink of water, milk, or juice.
- ¥ Listen to soft music.
- ¥ Talk to a trusted adult.
- ¥ Throw balls at a wall or rocks at a tin can (away from people).
- ¥ Count to a hundred (or backwards from 100).
- ¥ Take a walk outside and observe nature.
- ¥ Take a nap.

After the students have brainstormed ideas and you have added items from the above list, go through all the items and ask the students to think of the pros and cons of using each strategy. Next, invite the students to choose 3 to 5 anger control strategies to try out for themselves. Suggest that they include strategies that they have already found successful and new ones that they believe might be beneficial.

Give each student a 3" x 5" card, and ask the students to write down their chosen strategies. Tell them to call the list their Bag of Tricks.   Explain to the students that their task is to field test their Bag of Tricks over the next few weeks, trying each strategy in several situations. Ask the students to carry their card with them to serve as a reminder. Suggest that they mark the strategies that worked best for them and jot notes on the back of the card. Alert the students that some strategies may work in one situation and not in others, and strategies that work for one person may not work for everyone. Each Bag of Tricks will become individualized with time and practice.

Each week ask volunteers to report on their Bag of Tricks. Frequently remind the students that anger-control strategies are just short term controls, not permanent solutions to big problems. As field-test data are brought in and shared, summarize the information on a big chart. Eventually the students will be able to see graphically which strategies work best. Post the chart in the room.

Taking Control of Anger
Becoming Aware of Anger Reactions

Objectives:

The students will:

understand that anger is normal and that they can learn to control their reactions to anger.

become familiar with a range of typical responses to anger.

observe and evaluate their own behaviors in anger-provoking situations.

Materials:

one copy of the experience sheet, Chart Your Anger, for each student

Procedure:

Begin by telling the students a real story about a recent time when you got angry. For example, you might say:

I hope you don t mind if I share this with you. I was waiting in a line of cars to get on the freeway this morning and this person zoomed by me on the shoulder of the onramp. He was going so fast it looked like he was going to lose control of his car. He passed up all of us who were waiting patiently for our turn. I was furious. In fact, I still feel mad when I talk about it.

Ask the students if they ever get angry. Talk a little about the kinds of things that provoke anger in them.

Ask the students to take out a sheet of paper (or distribute paper) and write a list of events or situations that make them angry. Give the students 5 or 10 minutes to do this. When they have finished, tell them to go back through their list and number the items from Most Angry (#1) to Least Angry (highest number).

Next, return to your earlier story and talk about your behaviors when you were angry. Continuing with the previous example, you might say:

86

When I was angry with that driver this morning, I started yelling. No one could hear me inside my car, but I was yelling anyway. The woman in front of me laid on her horn, and I heard a couple of other horns blaring, too.

Explain that you and the other people were expressing your anger or blowing off steam. Point out that some ways of expressing anger are more effective than others. Also, some exhibit more self-control than others. Give the students an opportunity to talk about ways in which they express anger.

Then, have the students turn their sheet of paper over and, on the back, list things they do when they are angry. Give them another 5 to 10 minutes to complete this second list. When they have finished, tell them to go back through the list and number the items from Most Effective (#1) to Least Effective (highest number).

Ask volunteers to share their lists with the class. Discuss the effects of various expressions of anger, and the relative amounts of self-control they require.

Distribute the experience sheets. Go over the directions and answer any questions about the use of the chart. Explain that the students are to chart their reactions to anger for 1 week. Name a specific due date.

On the scheduled due date, have the students discuss their charts in small groups. Suggest that they take turns sharing one or two events from their chart. Talk about which behaviors worked for them and which didn t. Conclude the activity with a class discussion.

Discussion Questions:

1. What similarities did you notice in the things that made us angry?
2. What were the most common reactions?
3. What are the benefits of being in control?
4. What are the dangers of reacting with low self-control?
5. What high self-control behavior would you like to learn? How can you go about learning it?

87

Chart Your Anger!
Experience Sheet

Getting angry is a reaction that comes naturally. You hardly ever have to think about it. Here is what you do have to think about: How to control yourself when you are angry and how to express your anger in constructive ways. That s much harder.

Use the chart provided for one week. Every time you get angry, write it down. In the EVENT column, describe what happened to make you angry. In the REACTION column, put the number of the reaction that comes closest to what you did. Choose from the list below. If you did two or more things, put two or more numbers. At the end of the week, answer the questions on the other side. Then, bring your experience sheet back to class.

Reactions

Low Self-Control

1. Physically hurt someone.
2. Damage or destroy property.
3. Use alcohol or drugs to forget about it.
4. Yell accusations or threats.
5. Call a person lots of bad names.
6. Try to get someone in trouble by telling.
7. Ignore it and pretend nothing happened.
8. Take several deep breaths.
9. Count to ten.
10. Punch a pillow or a punching bag.
11. Assertively say what you think.
12. Go for a bike ride, or play a sport or game.
13. Listen to music.
14. Take a walk, run, or swim.
15. Do a relaxation exercise or meditation.
16. Write about it in your diary or journal.
17. Share your feelings with someone you trust.

High Self-Control

88

EVENT	REACTION

Questions:

1. Were any of the things that made you angry preventable? How? _____

_____

2. Which high self-control actions work best for you?_____

_____

3. Which high self-control actions would you like to learn? _____

_____

89

Control Yourself!
Building Self-Management Skills

Objectives:

The students will:

    identify different types of self-control and self-management behaviors.

    demonstrate behaviors associated with self-control in a variety of situations.

    publicly affirm how they feel about their own levels of self-control.

Materials:

chalkboard and chalk

Procedure:

Begin this session by asking the students what the term *self-control* means. Listen to and reflect the students responses. In the process, establish that having self-control means being able to restrain and regulate one s own behavior. Then say:

Think of a time when your emotions were so strong that you couldn t control yourself. Maybe you didn t want to cry or yell or laugh, but the feelings were overpowering.

Invite volunteers to tell the class about their experiences. Ask one or two to act out their incidents, demonstrating exactly what happened.

Next, whisper one of the following situations to a volunteer and have that student act out the situation in pantomime (nonverbally). Have the class guess what is happening and identify the emotion that the student is trying to control.

    ¥ You just crashed your bike, banging your leg badly, in front of several other kids.

    ¥ You get back a paper that you worked very hard on. It s covered with red marks and graded C-.

    ¥ Walking home at dusk, you turn a corner and practically run right into a big skunk.

90

¥ While your teacher is explaining an assignment, you see another student do something hysterically funny and try to keep from breaking up.

¥ Your parent restricts you for something your brother or sister did.

¥ You are walking home alone after just learning that a boy or girl you have a crush on likes you, too.

Repeat this process with the remainder of the situations and a new volunteer each time. After each pantomime, talk about methods typically used to control reactions to various emotions (biting tongue, clenching fists, taking deep breaths, blinking, stiffening muscles, looking away, etc.)

Draw a long horizontal line across the board. At one end write Volcanic Vicki. At the other end write, Restrained Robert. Explain to the students that the line is a *self-control continuum* and that Vicki and Robert represent the extreme endpoints. Ask the students to help you describe Vicki and Robert. Have fun with this and encourage the students to exaggerate their descriptions. For example:

Volcanic Vicki is going off all the time. At the slightest provocation, steam spews from her nostrils, tears form her eyes, and agonizing, earth shaking sounds from her throat. Vicki was once able to control herself for 20 seconds, and that was when a bee landed on her nose.

Restrained Robert looks a little like an automated store mannequin. His expression almost never changes and his movements are stiff and controlled. People have exhausted themselves trying to make Robert laugh, or blink, or get angry. But Robert would rather die than lose control.

Ask two or three students at a time to write their names somewhere on the continuum. Explain that before they do this, they must decide how much self-control they have. Are they closer to Vicki s end of the continuum or Robert s? Give all of the students an opportunity to place themselves on the line.

Lead a culminating class discussion, focusing on the concepts of self-control and self-management. Then, with the last few minutes remaining, play a little game with the students. Tell them to sit absolutely still without

(Continued)

fidgeting, talking, or blinking. Explain that the last student to move is the winner. Time the students and proclaim the winner, Self-control King or Self-control Queen for the day.

Discussion Questions:

1. Why is it important to learn self-control?
2. What would school be like if students and teachers never made any effort to manage their feelings or behavior?
3. What does self-management have to do with responsibility?
4. What do your parents mean when they tell you to be on your best behavior?
5. How do you feel when you successfully control yourself?

Variation:

With younger students, draw an imaginary self-control line on the floor and have the children stand in the spot that represents their place on the continuum. Have two students act out the parts of Volcanic Vicki and Restrained Robert while standing at either end of the imaginary line.